AF751637

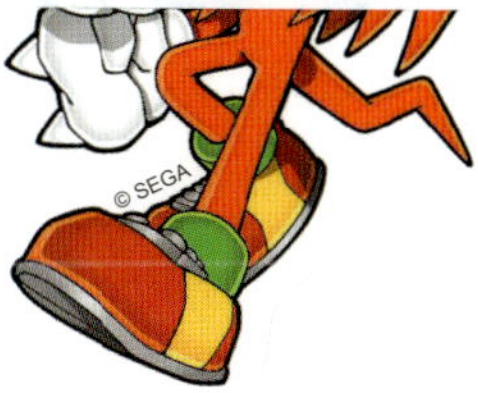

SONIC™
THE HEDGEHOG
WELCOME TO THE
WORLD
OF
SONIC

Published by Scholastic Australia in 2024.

Scholastic Australia Pty Limited
PO Box 579 Gosford NSW 2250
ABN 11 000 614 577
www.scholastic.com.au

Part of the Scholastic Group

Sydney • Auckland • New York • Toronto • London • Mexico City
New Delhi • Hong Kong • Buenos Aires • Puerto Rico

ISBN 978-1-76152-970-2

Printed in China.

Scholastic Australia's policy, in association with its printers, is to use papers that are renewable and made efficiently from wood grown in responsibly managed forests, so as to minimise its environmental footprint.

SONIC™ THE HEDGEHOG

WELCOME TO THE WORLD OF SONIC

by Lloyd Cordill

TABLE OF CONTENTS

Hey there, speedster!

Nice of you to stop by.
It's me, Sonic--Sonic the Hedgehog!
I've had quite a few adventures in my day
and met a host of wacky characters, including
the occasional vile, villainous villain. How many of my
adventures do YOU remember?

Today, I thought I'd take a leisurely stroll (at 2,000
miles per hour) down memory lane and revisit some of
my coolest and most epic adventures.
So come along with me. Let's
see if you can keep up!

CHARACTERS

CHARACTERS

SONIC THE HEDGEHOG

Stats:

Species: Hedgehog

Gender: Male

Weight: 77 lbs.

Height: 3 feet, 4 inches

Status: Fastest thing alive

Who am I?

I'm Sonic, the fastest thing you've ever seen. It's no coincidence that I'm the star of the show, because I'm the coolest, the toughest, the best-- and the most modest.

I love hanging out in nature and living by my own rules. I try to mind my own business, but when I see cute animals in trouble, I can't help myself--I have to help. If Dr. Eggman gets in my way, you can bet there'll be hedgehog to pay.

Tails' Trivia

By what alliterative alias is Sonic known?

A) The Hasty Hedgehog

B) The Fast Furzepig

C) The Blue Blur

D) The Blue Bolt

SONIC IN COMBAT

Not only am I fast, but when the going gets tough, I get fighting! I've had to face more than a few giant robots on my adventures. Dr. Eggman can't seem to take a hint. And I've picked up more than a few signature moves from all those battles.

Spin Dash

My Spin Dash attack is a lot like throwing a baseball. First the wind up, then the pitch! When I want to pick up speed before I start rolling, I'll crouch into a ball and spin in a circle. When I let loose, everyone better get out of my way, because my quills will cut sharper than a buzz saw.

Homing Attack

When I'm in midair, I can zero in on an enemy and perform a Homing Attack. I can lock on to an enemy robot and knock 'em right in the bolts. I'm like a heat-seeking missile! Except I'm blue, and a hedgehog.

Super Sonic

With the power of the Chaos Emeralds, I can become Super Sonic! Super Me is just like Regular Me, except way more powerful and way more yellow.

SONIC STYLE

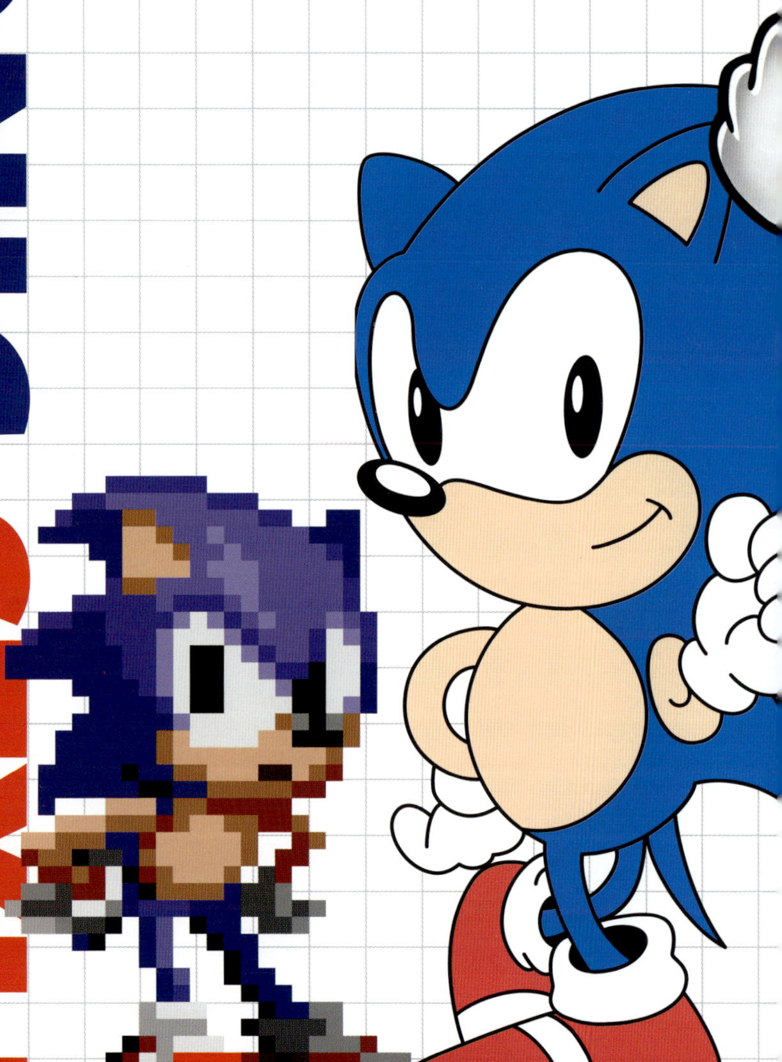

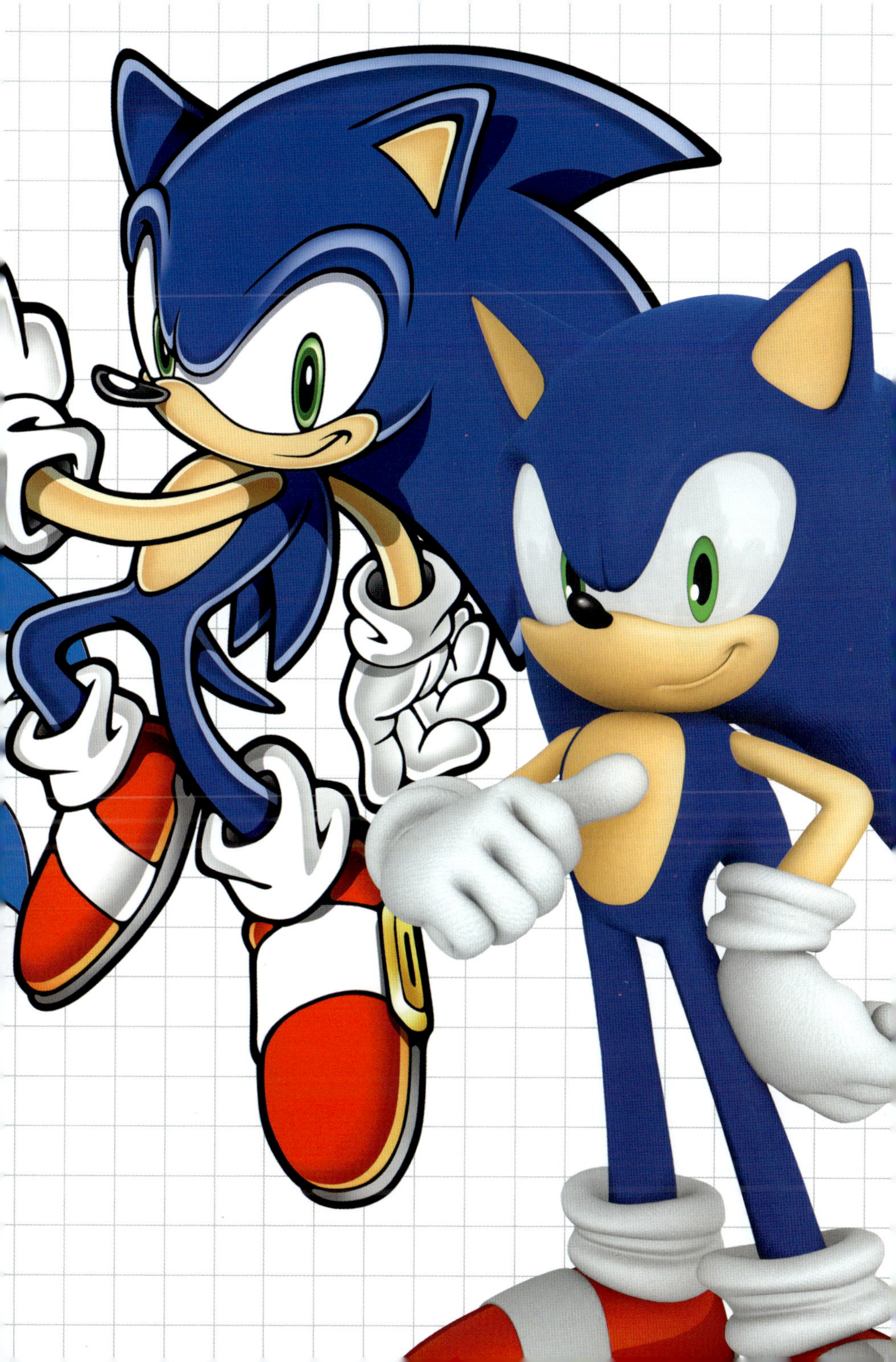

TAILS

MILES "TAILS" PROWER

Stats:

Species: Fox

Gender: Male

Weight: 44 lbs.

Height: 2 feet, 4 inches

Status: Sonic's best friend

and have even joined the battle when my best buddy Sonic was in a jam.
I've gone on a few adventures of my own, too!
What is the name of Sonic's red-and-white biplane that Tails likes to fly?
A) Hurricane
B) Tails' Traveler
C) The Red Baron
D) Tornado
Tails' Trivia

KNUCKLES
THE ECHIDNA

Stats:

Species: Echidna

Gender: Male

Weight: 88 lbs.

Height: 3 feet, 4 inches

Status: Sonic's good friend and rival

I'm Knuckles the Echidna,

and with my spiky knuckles and superhuman strength, I can climb over any obstacle. People say I'm gullible, but I'll never again believe Sonic when he tells me my shoe is untied. Not one more time!

My sworn duty on Angel Island is to protect the Master Emerald. I won't be distracted. That said, whenever a friend is in danger, you can count on me to dig to the rescue.

FLOATING ISLAND

Knuckles was born and raised on a beautiful island that floats high in the clouds. The island contains many different environments, like sandy deserts, snow-capped mountains, and lush forests. Knuckles is the guardian of the Master Emerald, which is the source of the island's floating power. Without the Master Emerald, the island would fall into the ocean.

MASTER EMERALD

The Master Emerald is a gem of phenomenal power that can balance the power of the Chaos Emeralds if they get out of control. Knuckles is sworn to keep the Master Emerald safe.

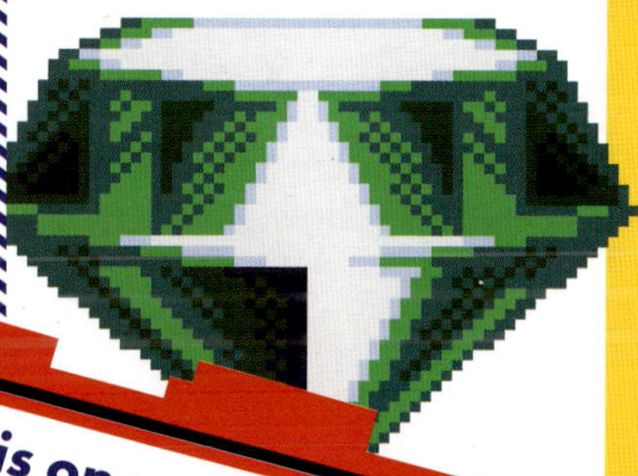

Which of these is one of Knuckles' special talents?

A) snowboarding

B) treasure hunting

C) juggling

D) changing the weather

Tails' Trivia

AMY

AMY ROSE

Stats:

Species: Hedgehog

Gender: Female

Weight: Not telling!

Height: 2 feet, 11 inches

Status: Sonic's admirer

Hiya, I'm Amy!

Isn't that Sonic so dreamy? Sigh . . . If I can ever get him to slow down, we might be able to go on a date someday.

Which is one of Amy's hobbies?

A) figure skating
B) reading Tarot cards
C) writing poetry
D) playing checkers

SHADOW THE HEDGEHOG

Stats:

Species: Hedgehog

Gender: Male

Weight: 77 lbs.

Height: 3 feet, 4 inches

Status: Unknown

PROJECT SHADOW

Dr. Eggman's grandfather, Professor Gerald Robotnik, attempted to use Project Shadow to create a formula capable of achieving immortality. He wanted to save Maria, his granddaughter. The project resulted in the creation of Shadow the Hedgehog, among other things.

Tails' Trivia

What is the name of the space colony where Shadow was created?

A) Jupiter

B) Comet II

C) ARK

D) Biolizard

SILVER THE HEDGEHOG

Stats:

Species: Hedgehog

Gender: Male

Weight: 77 lbs.

Height: 3 feet, 4 inches

Status: Sonic's friend

Time-traveling hedgehog, Silver, here.

When I first met Sonic, I thought he had destroyed my world, so I went into the past to defeat him. But then I realized that he was trying to save *the world, just like me. We worked together and saved the day. Now I help Sonic and his other friends fight the good fight and set things right.*

What word describes Silver's ability to lift heavy objects and levitate with just his mind?

A) telemetry

B) telekinesis

C) telephone

D) televation

Tails' Trivia

BLAZE THE CAT

Stats:

Species: Cat

Gender: Female

Weight: Unknown

Height: 3 feet, 2 inches

Status: Cream's best friend, ally of Sonic

Hello there, scholar. It is I, Blaze the Cat.

As you may have suspected from my previous statement, I am indeed a cat. I am also an imperial princess from a parallel dimension, and protector of the Sol Emeralds. I am sworn to carry the burden of these unique emeralds, which are similar in many respects to the Chaos Emeralds. I will use my fire powers to defeat all enemies. Come at me!

Blaze appears in Sonic and the Black Knight as which Knight of the Round Table?

A) Percival

B) Gawain

C) Lancelot

D) Sparkster

Tails' Trivia

CREAM
THE RABBIT

Stats:

Species: Rabbit

Gender: Female

Weight: 26 lbs.

Height: 2 feet, 4 inches

Status: Blaze's best friend, Sonic's pal

Who wants ice cream? I am Cream.

Thanks for coming to talk with me. I see you just met my friend Blaze. But have you met my buddy Cheese? He's a Chao! My mother is Vanilla. When my friends are in danger, I can swoop in to help by flapping my ears like big wings. People say I'm sweet as cream, but I think I'm bold--like a big, bold flavor. Whoops! Careful where you step. I dropped some ice cream over there.

Cheese is a child Chao and Cream's best friend. They often work together to attack enemies. Cheese can fly through the air and launch himself like a missile. With his stylish bow tie, Cheese is always ready for action.

Tails' Trivia

What is the name of Cheese's sibling?

A) Vanilla

B) Chocola

C) Straberrino

D) Mac

VECTOR
THE CROCODILE

Stats:

Species: Crocodile

Gender: Male

Weight: 440 lbs.

Height: 5 feet, 11 inches

Status: Leader of Chaotix Detective Agency

Aw yeah, time to rock out!

I'm Vector, the leader of Chaotix and founding member of our detective agency. Some people say I can be a bit gruff and hot-headed (and that's true!) but you won't find a crocodile who cares more about his fellow animals and doing the right thing.

Tails' Trivia

What surprising role did Dr. Eggman play in the Chaotix Detective Agency's story in Sonic Heroes?

A) He was their partner.

B) He was their landlord.

C) He was their cab driver.

D) He was their client.

CHARMY

CHARMY BEE

Stats:

Species: Bee

Gender: Male

Weight: 22 lbs.

Height: 2 feet, 4 inches

Status: Member of Chaotix

Bee serious, you're suprised to see me.

Tails' Trivia

While aboard the Space Colony ARK, Charmy saved the world by sticking his stinger into what?

A) a door

B) a rocket

C) a computer

D) Dr. Eggman

ESPIO
THE CHAMELEON

Stats:

Species: Chameleon

Gender: Male

Weight: 80 lbs.

Height: 3 feet, 8 inches

Status: Member of Chaotix

Espio here, detective and ninja.

Do not expect me to speak at great length, for it is my role as a silent and stealthy individual to speak only when necessary. Am I the brains of Team Chaotix? I'll never tell, but as a master of ninjutsu I can assure you that I am a valued member of our detective agency.

Who helped Espio when he sneaked into the Mad Matrix?

A) Sonic

B) Knuckles

C) Charmy Bee

D) Shadow

Tails' Trivia

ROUGE
THE BAT

Stats:

Species: Bat

Gender: Female

Weight: Unknown

Height: 3 feet, 6 inches

Status: Friend of Knuckles

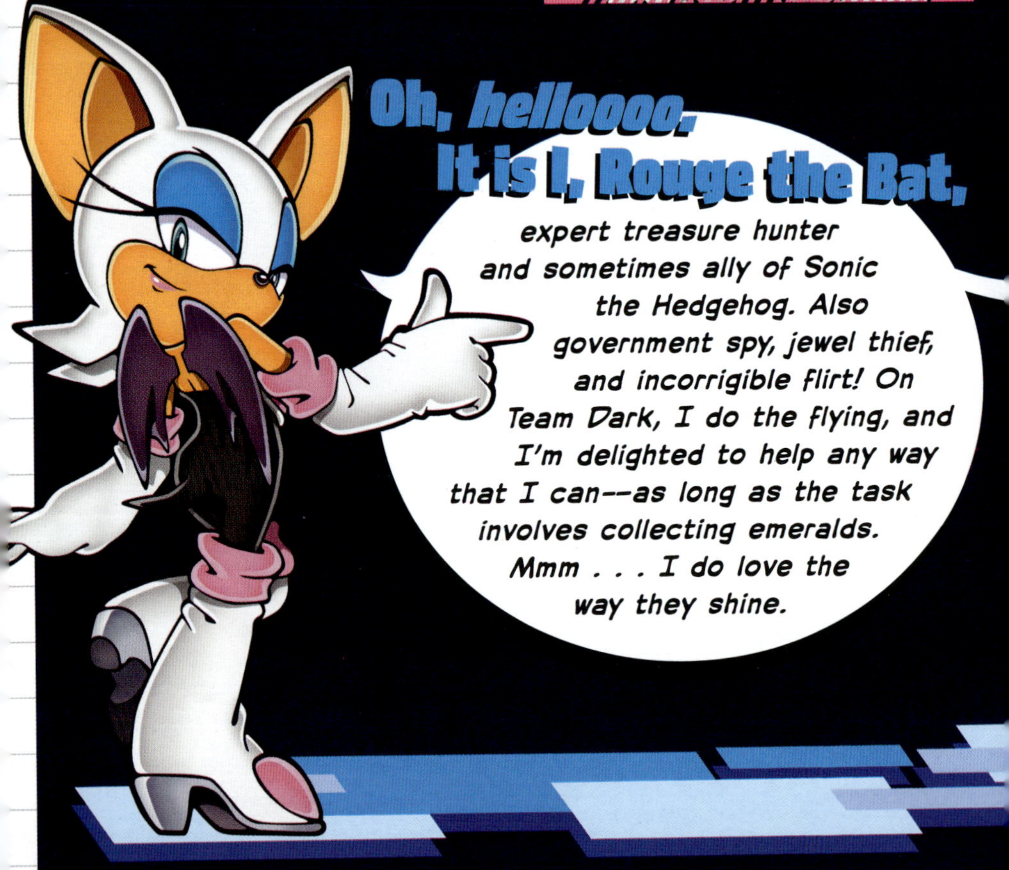

I often work as an agent-for-hire for the Guardian Units of Nations, or G.U.N., who answer to the president of the United Federation. When robot beetles and other high-powered weapons can't do the job, I'll step in and provide a more delicate hand.

Under G.U.N.'s orders, Rouge was once sent to steal the Scepter of ____?

A) Darkness

B) Speed

C) Style

D) Sandwiches

Tails' Trivia

CHAO

Stats:

Species: Chao

Gender: N/A

Weight: 15 lbs.

Height: 1 foot, 4 inches

Status: Adorable

Tails' Trivia

The places where Chao are raised are called ______.

A) Chao Gardens
B) Chao Villages
C) Chao Incubators
D) Chao Nurseries

Dr. EGGMAN

EVIL GENIUS

Stats:

Species: Human

Gender: Male

Weight: 282 lbs.

Height: 6 feet, 2 inches

Status: Stupid genius supervillain

Attention, losers! Heed my words!

It is I, Dr. Eggman, corpulent scientific genius and sworn enemy of Sonic the Hedgehog. Whether building a mechanical army by turning cuddly animals into deadly robots, or constructing massive machines capable of wreaking havoc on an unsuspecting populace, I have been nipping at Sonic's speedy heels since the very beginning! One day I will achieve my goals . . . I just don't know when!

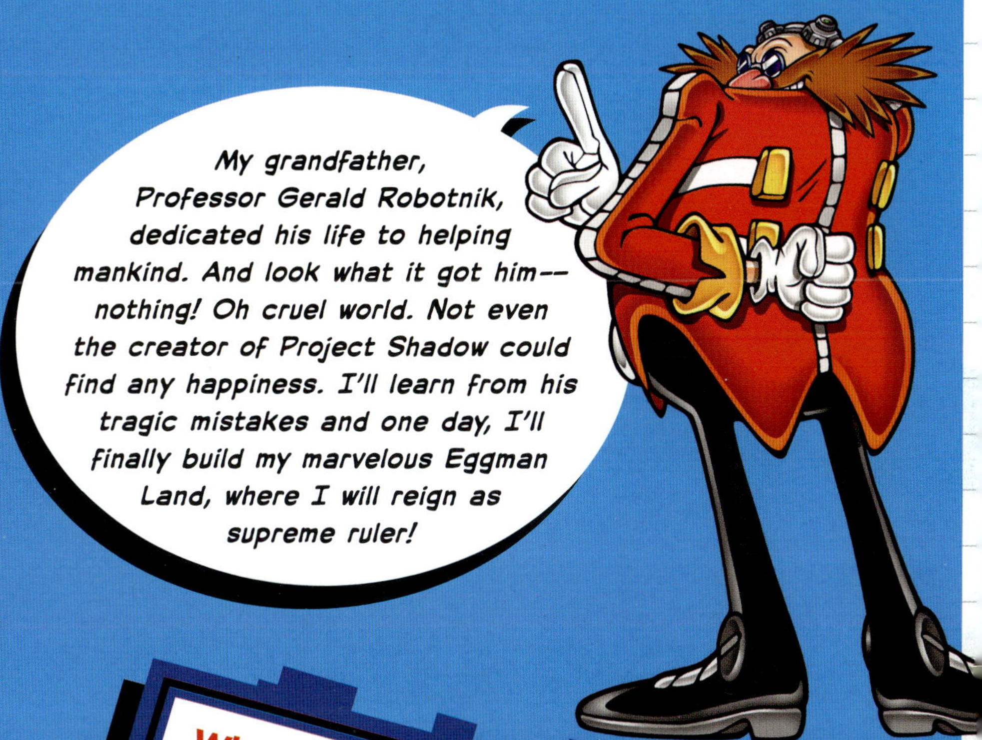

Tails' Trivia

What is the name of Eggman's flying fortress?

A) The Robotnikopter
B) The Eggcellent Aeroplane
C) The Egg Carrier
D) The Mustache Blimp

E-102
GAMMA

Stats:

Species: Robot

Gender: N/A

Weight: 1,818 lbs.

Height: 7 feet

Status: Gun-toting fighting machine

CLASSIFIED DOCUMENT

Aberration detected. Due to enormous willpower in an unusually strong bird, unit E-102 Gamma went rogue and betrayed master robot builder Dr. Eggman. After meeting female hedgehog "Amy Rose," E-102 Gamma became self-aware and embarked on a bird rescue mission.

CLASSIFIED DOCUMENT (continued)

The traitorous Gamma hunted down and destroyed his brothers, but was fatally damaged in a climactic battle with E-101 Beta. E-102 Gamma was destroyed. The location of the bird that was once inside Gamma is currently unknown.

Tails' Trivia

What color was the little bird trapped inside E-102 Gamma?

A) red

B) white

C) blue

D) pink

BIG THE CAT

Stats:

Species: Cat

Gender: Male

Weight: 616 lbs.

Height: 6 feet, 8 inches

Status: Feline fisherman

Froggy, is that you?

I hope you haven't eaten my lucky charm, the yellow Chaos Emerald, again!

I'm Big the Cat, a happy fisherman cat. I spend most of my time hanging out in the Mystic Ruins, but when Froggy the Frog hops off, I'll travel all over the world to find him.

Like most cats, I love fish! I'd be happy sittin' and fishin' all day long. One time, I teamed up with Amy and Cream to find Froggy and Cheese's twin, Chocola. I'd rather not fight anybody, but I'll do what I need to do to keep Froggy out of trouble. I may not be the brightest cat in the world, but I love my Froggy, and I'd do anything to help him.
Big the Cat, Amy, and Cream the Rabbit make up what adventuring squad?
A) Team Mammals
B) Team Rose
C) Team Sweet
D) Team Cream Cheese
Tails' Trivia

BABYLON ROGUES

JET THE HAWK

Stats:
Species: Hawk
Gender: Male
Weight: 73 lbs.
Height: 3 feet, 4 inches
Status: Leader of the Babylon Rogues

WAVE THE SWALLOW

Stats:
Species: Swallow
Gender: Female
Weight: Secret
Height: 3 feet, 8 inches
Status: Member of the Babylon Rogues

STORM THE ALBATROSS

Stats:
Species: Albatross
Gender: Male
Weight: 176 lbs.
Height: 4 feet, 8 inches
Status: Member of the Babylon Rogues

Are you a fellow rider? I'm Jet.

Along with my mates Wave the Swallow and Storm the Albatross, we are the Babylon Rogues, a group of treasure-minded spelunkers who have been around in one form or another since ancient times. We've been known to work with anyone who can lead us to treasure, even Dr. Eggman! I'm happy to go toe-to-talon with Sonic any day of the week. He better watch out!

We are masters of Extreme Gear! We can zoom faster than anyone out there. Who's Sonic? Sounds like a slow name. We are fast, we are cool, we are the Babylon Rogues!

Each member of the Babylon Rogues is a descendent of what?

A) hawks

B) ancient Babylonians

C) gardeners

D) snowboarders

Tails' Trivia

CHAOS

Stats:

Species: Chao (mutated)

Gender: Unknown

Weight: Unknown

Height: Unknown

Status: Dangerous

Not this bozo!

When Dr. Eggman broke the Master Emerald, Chaos awoke. At first he kind of looked like when you squeeze a tube of toothpaste into the sink, but every time I faced him, he absorbed another Chaos Emerald, making Chaos stronger and stronger.

Tails' Trivia

How did Sonic finally defeat Chaos?

A) Sonic challenged Chaos to a swing-dancing competition.
B) Sonic flew the Tornado into Chaos.
C) Sonic turned into Super Sonic.
D) Sonic teamed up with Dr. Eggman.

METAL SONIC
THE STEEL NEMESIS

Stats:

Species: Robot (Badnik)

Gender: N/A

Weight: 276 lbs.

Height: 3 feet, 4 inches

Status: Sonic's robot doppelgänger

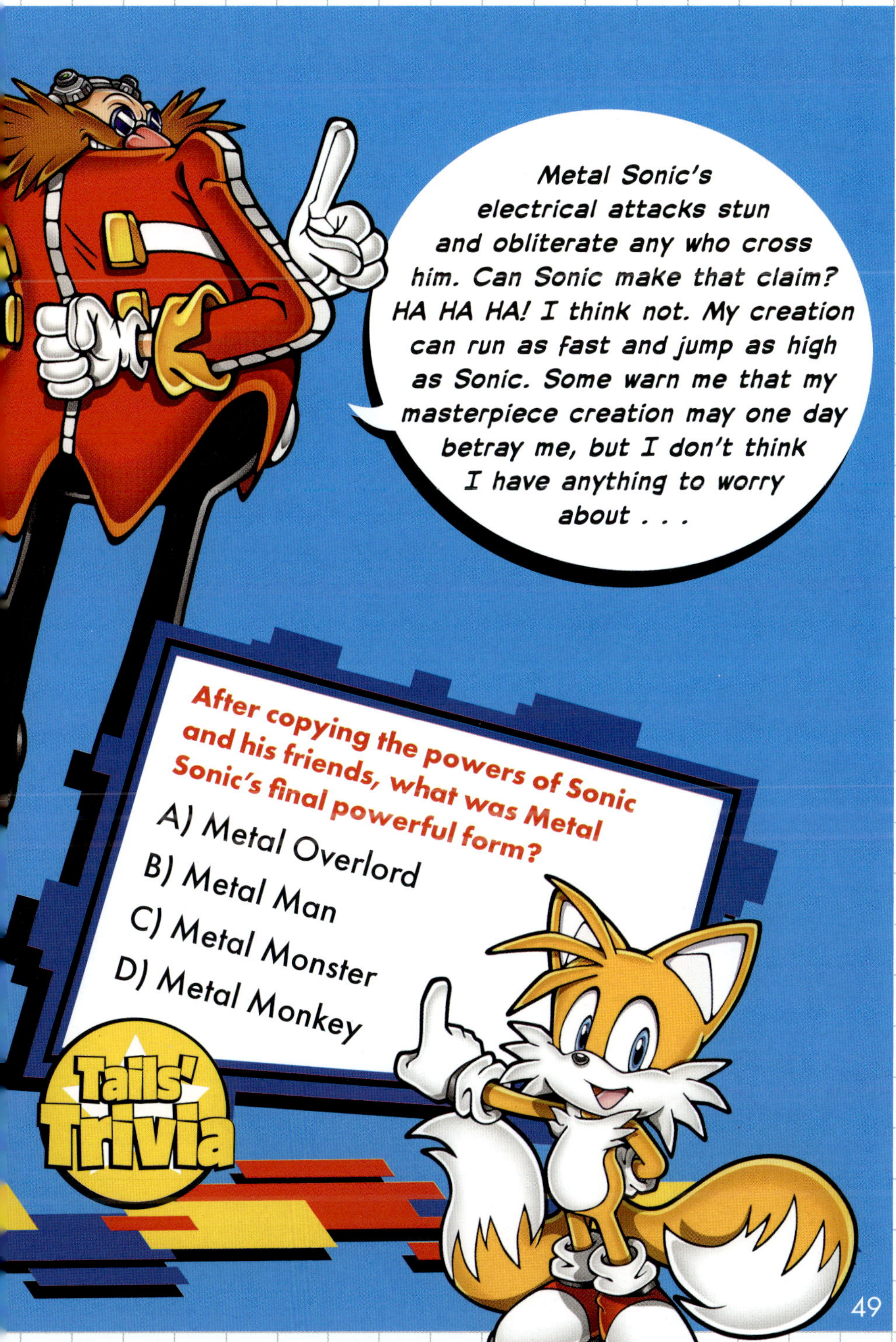
Metal Sonic's electrical attacks stun and obliterate any who cross him. Can Sonic make that claim? HA HA HA! I think not. My creation can run as fast and jump as high as Sonic. Some warn me that my masterpiece creation may one day betray me, but I don't think I have anything to worry about . . .
After copying the powers of Sonic and his friends, what was Metal Sonic's final powerful form?
A) Metal Overlord
B) Metal Man
C) Metal Monster
D) Metal Monkey
Tails' Trivia

STORIES

STORIES

SONIC ADVENTURE

SONIC ADVENTURE

Not long after that, the military came after me! And I had JUST saved the world.

Turned out, Shadow the Hedgehog had stolen a Chaos Emerald and they thought he was me. I don't know how they could have mixed up his grumpy face with mine!

Tails, Knuckles, Amy, and I had to scoop up all the emeralds we could. Then, Eggman threatened to blow everything up with the Eclipse Cannon. But I put a stop to Eggman, Shadow, and the cannon. You know, the usual!

SONIC ADVANCE 1–3

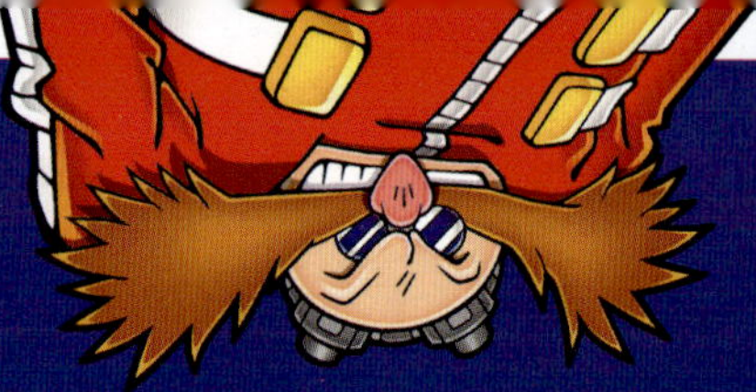

The next time Eggman tried to make a robot army, he kidnapped Tails and Knuckles. Luckily, Cheese and I were there to help Sonic out. Sonic attacked Eggman's Egg Utopia space station, where he rescued his friends, saved my mom Vanilla, and won the battle!

When Sonic and I got split up from our friends, we set out to find them and the missing Chaos Emeralds. As you can probably guess, Eggman sent a bunch of robots after us, but we faced one superpowerful robot named Gemerl and defeated it, saving the day!

SONIC HEROES

To defeat Metal Overlord, our teams of heroes needed to work together!

TEAM SONIC

SONIC | TAILS | KNUCKLES

TEAM ROSE
AMY
CREAM
BIG
TEAM DARK
SHADOW
ROUGE
OMEGA
TEAM CHAOTIX
ESPIO
CHARMY
VECTOR

SONIC RUSH

During one of Sonic's adventures, I made my grand entrance, arriving from another dimension in pursuit of the seven Sol Emeralds, which were stolen by Dr. Eggman.
I worked with Sonic and Cream to get the emeralds back. In the end, I transformed into Burning Blaze to defeat Dr. Eggman and his counterpart, Eggman Nega.

SONIC RUSH ADVENTURE

SONIC COLORS

Eggman said he'd turned over a new leaf and opened his Amazing Interstellar Amusement Park to make amends for his bad behavior.

But I knew THAT was too good to be true.

Tails and I learned that Eggman was really using the amusement park as a front to harvest the power of the local aliens, called Wisps. But we freed the planets Eggman had captured and saved the Wisps!

Five planets imprisoned by the Egg Mecha made up Dr. Eggman's Incredible Interstellar Amusement Park. Eggman's Ultra Accelerating Space Elevator carried people to and from the surface of our planet. The park was destroyed when one of Eggman's weapons made a black hole. Whoops!

SONIC GENERATIONS

Can't a hedgehog celebrate his own birthday in peace? There I was, minding my own business, when this freaky being known as the Time Eater showed up and transported all my friends to different points in my past.

I ended up in White Space, where I had to revisit past adventures (sound familiar?) and collect the Chaos Emeralds. Only by collecting the emeralds could I save my friends.

Along the way I met this little guy—he looked like me, but he actually came from another dimension!

SONIC GENERATIONS

Green Hill

Chemical Plant

Seaside Hill

Sky Sanctuary

SONIC LOST WORLD

When Eggman shot down the Tornado over the floating continent called Lost Hex, Tails and I had to rescue some helpless animals. Unfortunately, the Deadly Six had other plans. The Deadly Six were some real nasty demons that Eggman had enslaved with a magical seashell called the Cacophonous Conch.

The mad doctor's master plan was to use the Extractor to slurp up all the energy from our planet. We defeated the Deadly Six and Tails hacked the Extractor to undo what Eggman had done. We won the day once again.

THE DEADLY SIX

ZAVOK

THE LEADER

ZAZZ

THE CRAZY ONE

ZEENA

THE FEISTY ONE

MASTER ZIK

TEACHER OF ZAVOK

ZOMOM

THE HUNGRY ONE

ZOR

THE SNEAKY ONE

SONIC AND THE SECRET RINGS

I've always had a thing for picking up golden rings, but when I picked up this one ring, a genie named Shahra popped out of the Arabian Nights world. In Shahra's world, a nasty creep named Erazor Djinn was stealing the power of the Arabian Nights in an attempt to invade the real world.

To make matters worse, Erazor Djinn shot me with a flaming arrow. My life force would be snuffed out unless I could bring Erazor the seven World Rings, so I set out to find them.

I fought genies, giant scorpions, and zombies. I met Ali Baba and Sinbad. I battled across the land. When Erazor transformed into Alf Layla wa-Layla, I thought I was done for, but I transformed into Darkspine Sonic and defeated the djinn. It sure was a heck of an adventure. I still have sand in my shoes!

SONIC AND THE BLACK KNIGHT

The Black Knight was secretly King Arthur, who had been corrupted. He still held the scabbard of Excalibur, which made him immortal. I had to train in swordsmanship to face my opponents. And a smug talking sword helped me do it!

SONIC UNLEASHED

I was facing Eggman on his flagship in one of our biggest, most epic battles yet, when I turned into Super Sonic to finish the job. But Eggman had other plans.

He used his Chaos Energy Cannon to trap me, split our planet in half, and wake up Dark Gaia, who was one nasty dude.

Using the Chaos Emeralds, Eggman transformed me into a werehog--an enormous snarling and hairy version of myself. In this form, I met Chip, who turned out to be Light Gaia and helped me on my adventure.

In the end, Chip used the Gaia Temples to turn into Gaia Colossus, who actually stood a chance against the Perfect Dark Gaia. With Dark Gaia defeated, Chip flung us back to the surface where we were safe.

ALL-STAR RACING TRANSFORMED»»

THE END